# Read     Trace     Write

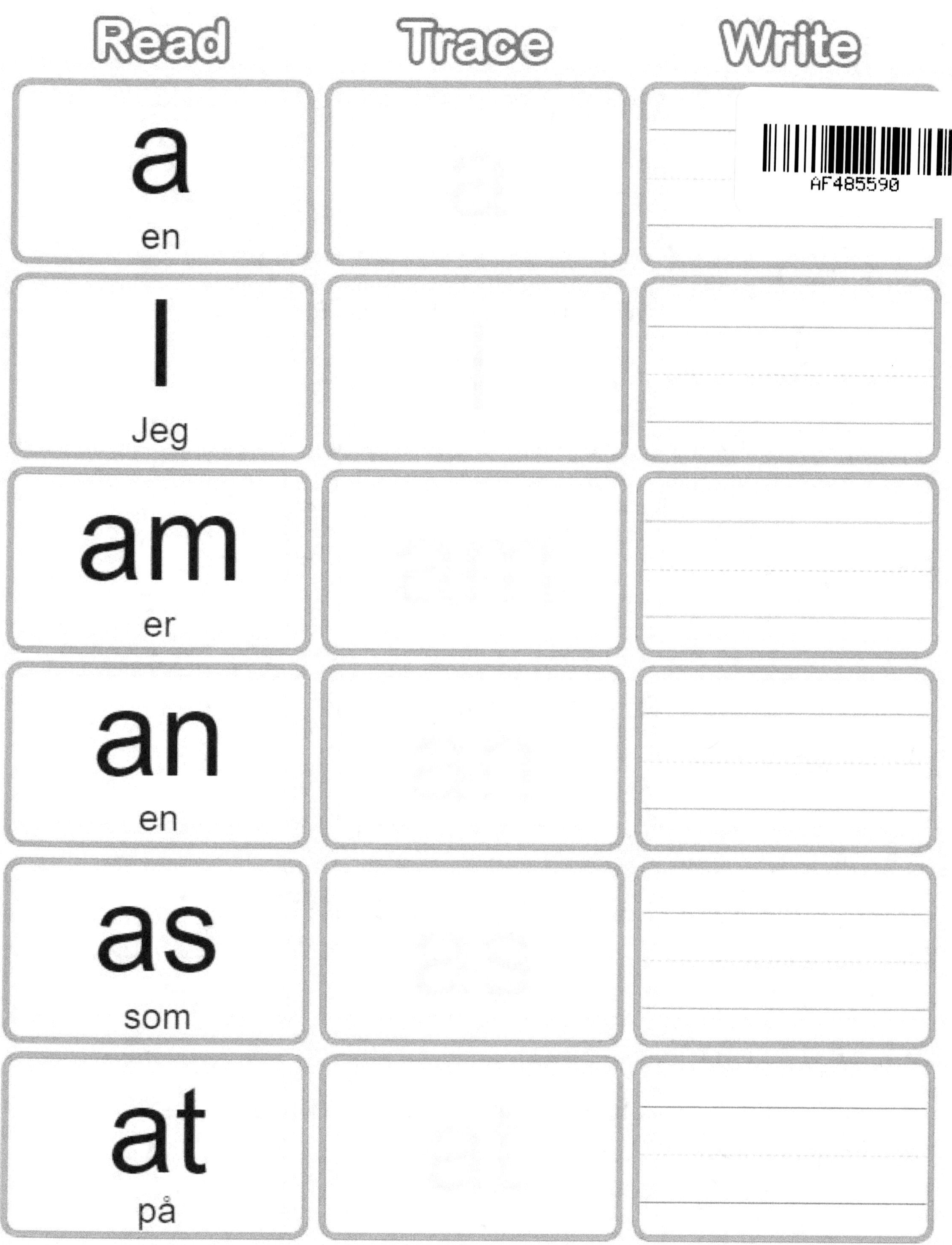

# Read and write the sentence!

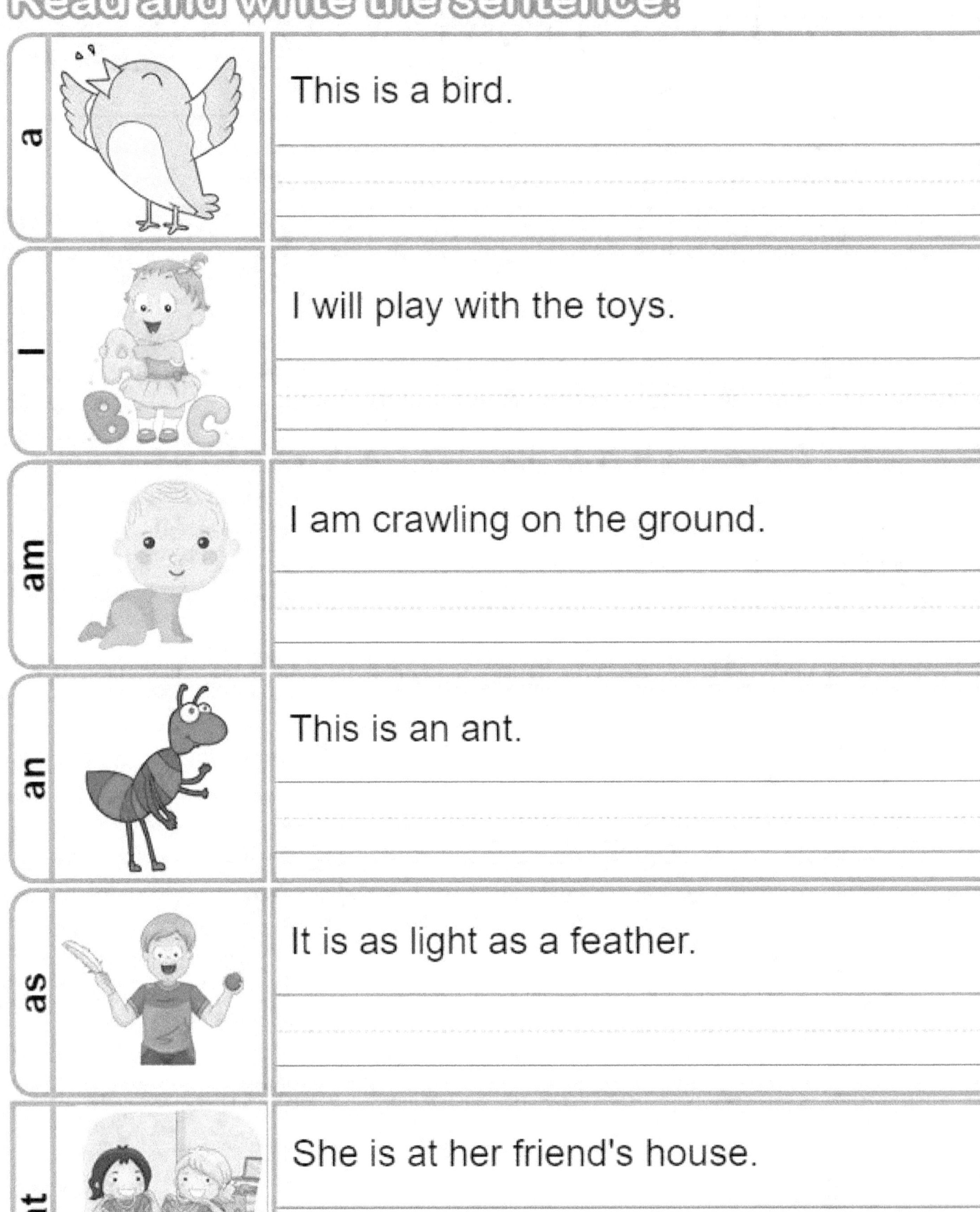

Read
Trace
Write
be
være
by
av
do
gjøre
go
gå
he
han
if
hvis

# Read and write the sentence!

| be | We will be friends. |
| by | This story is by me. |
| do | She will do the cleaning. |
| go | He will go somewhere. |
| he | He is bored. |
| if | If I put my clothes here, it will get washed. |

Read
Trace
Write
in
i
is
er
it
den
me
meg
my
min
no
nei

# Read and write the sentence!

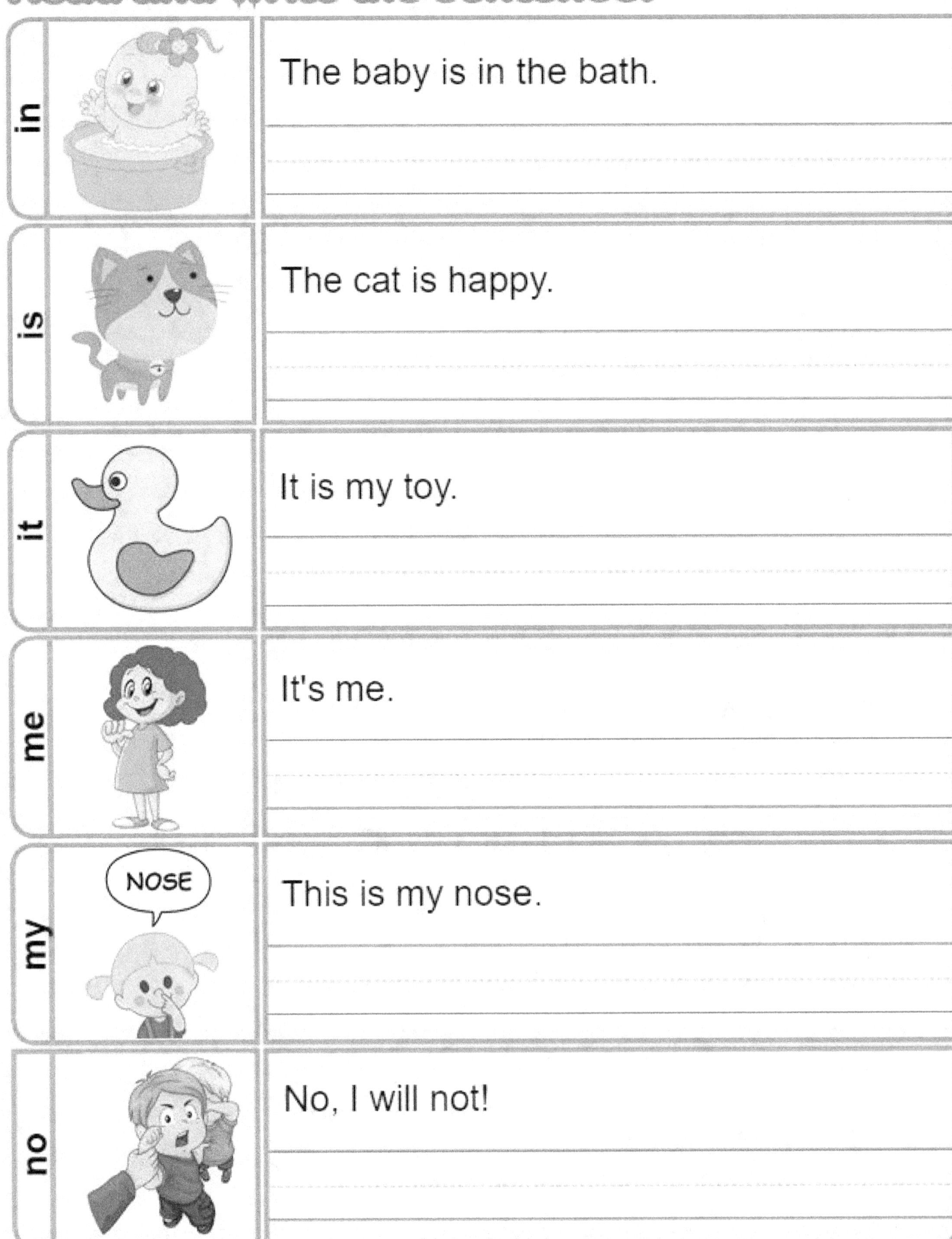

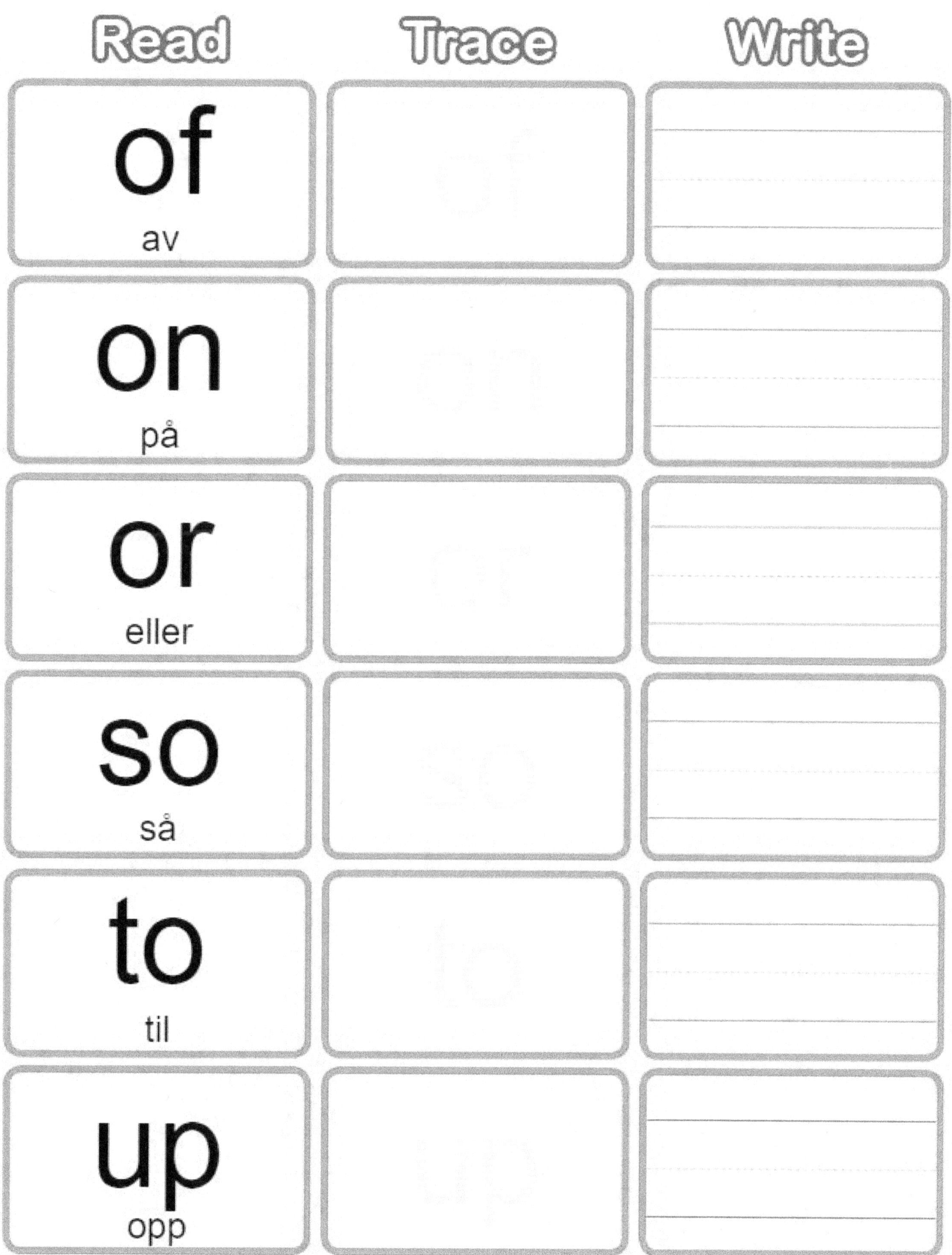

| Read | Trace | Write |
|---|---|---|
| of<br>av | | |
| on<br>på | | |
| or<br>eller | | |
| so<br>så | | |
| to<br>til | | |
| up<br>opp | | |

# Read and write the sentence!

Read
Trace
Write

us
oss

we
vi

all
alle

and
og

any
noen

are
er

# Read and write the sentence!

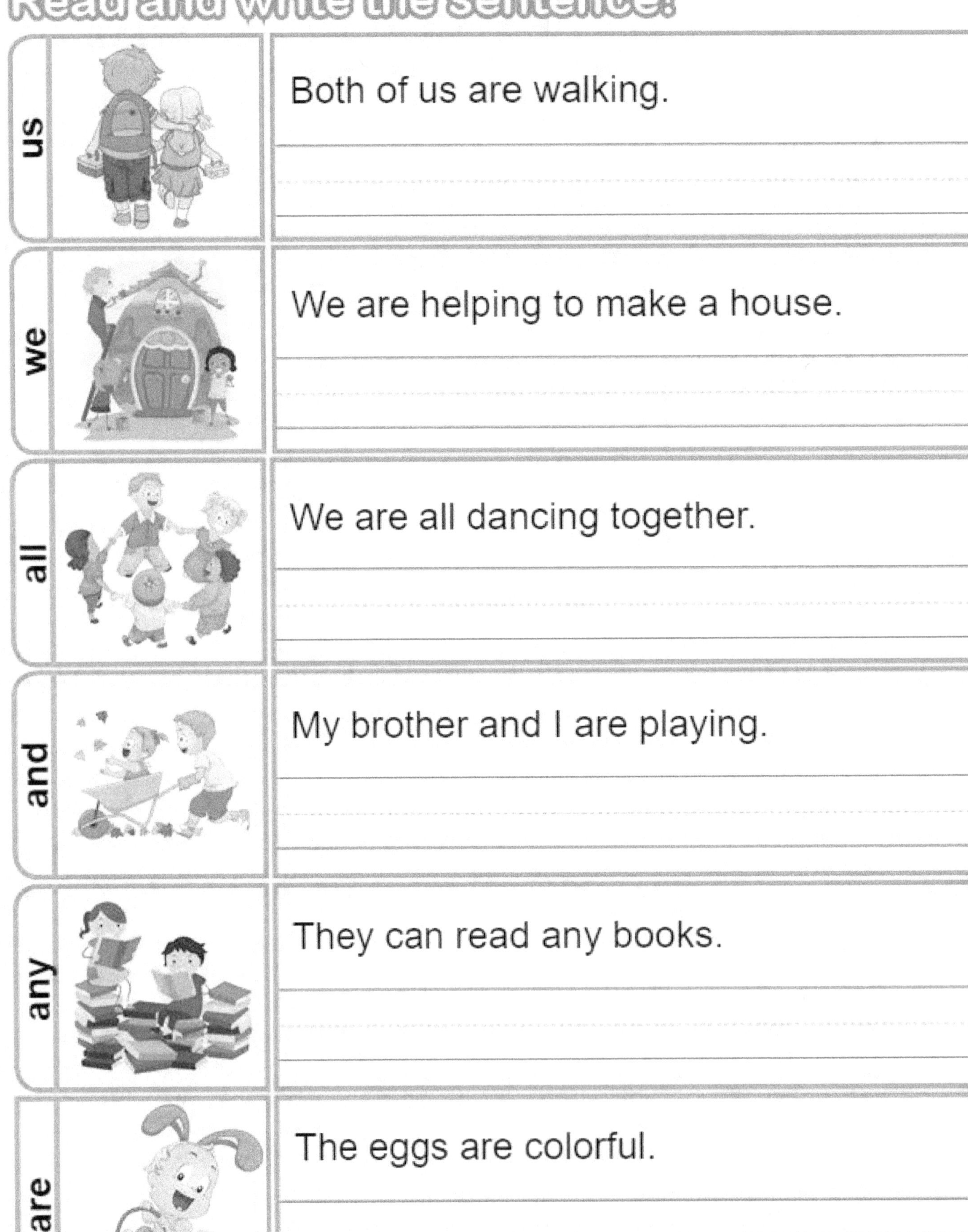

Read
Trace
Write
ask
spørre
ate
spiste
bed
seng
big
stor
box
eske
boy
gutt

# Read and write the sentence!

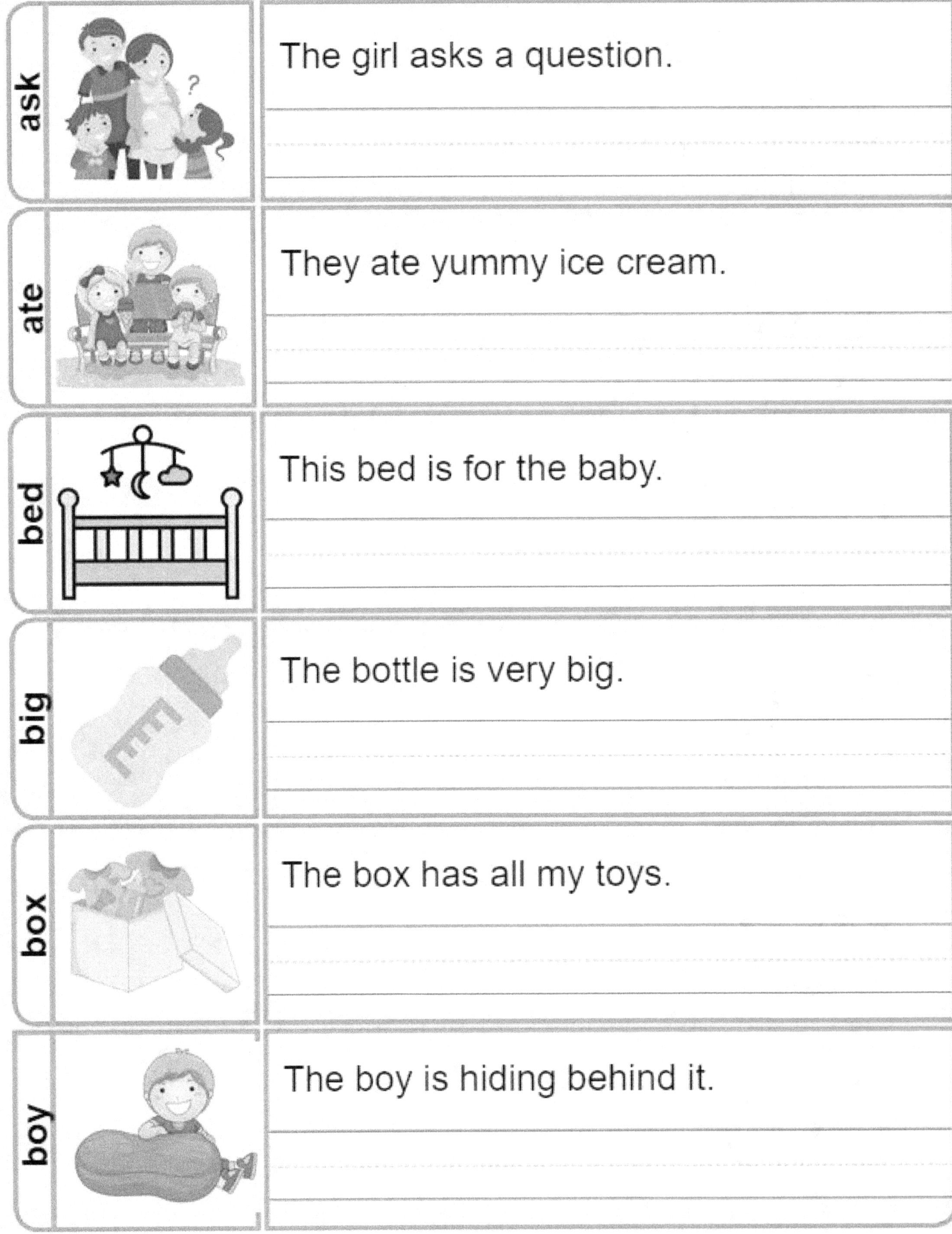

Read
Trace
Write
but
men
buy
kjøpe
can
kan
car
bil
cat
katt
cow
ku

# Read and write the sentence!

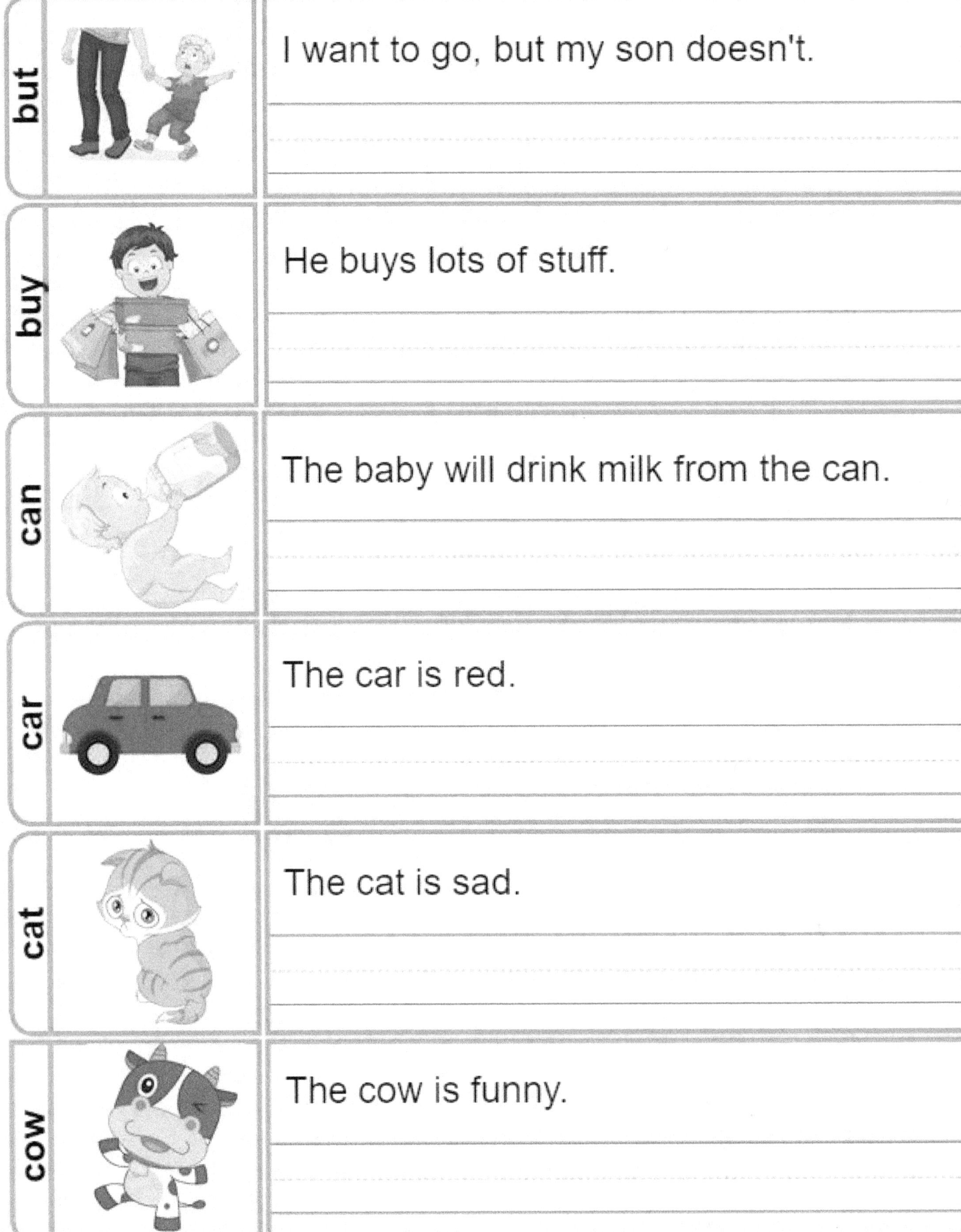

| but | I want to go, but my son doesn't. |
| buy | He buys lots of stuff. |
| can | The baby will drink milk from the can. |
| car | The car is red. |
| cat | The cat is sad. |
| cow | The cow is funny. |

Read
Trace
Write
cut
kutte opp
day
dag
did
gjorde
dog
hund
eat
spise
egg
egg

# Read and write the sentence!

Read
Trace
Write
eye
øye
far
langt
fly
fly
for
til
get
få
got
fikk

# Read and write the sentence!

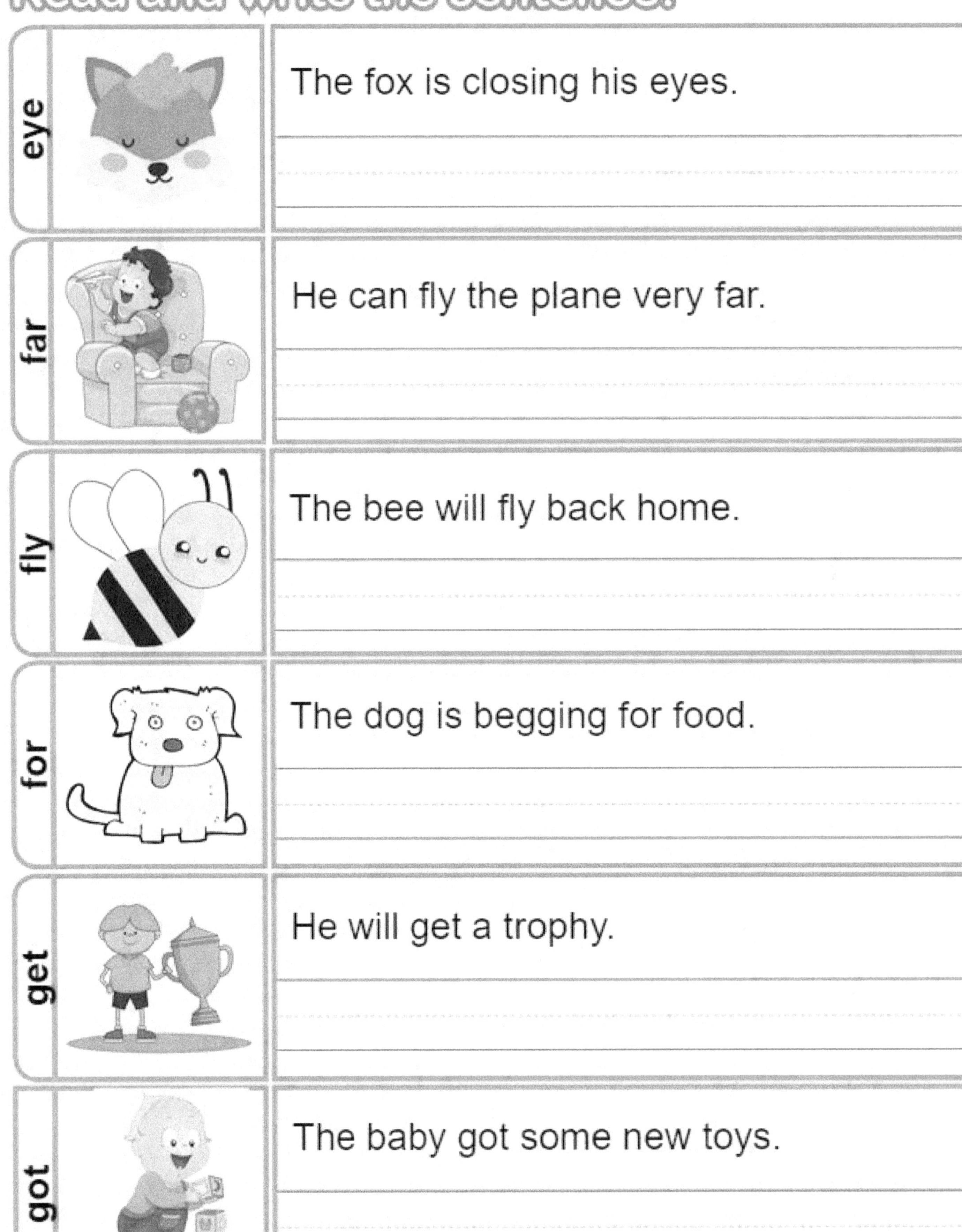

| Read | Trace | Write |
| --- | --- | --- |
| had<br>hadde | | |
| has<br>har | | |
| her<br>henne | | |
| him<br>ham | | |
| his<br>hans | | |
| hot<br>varmt | | |

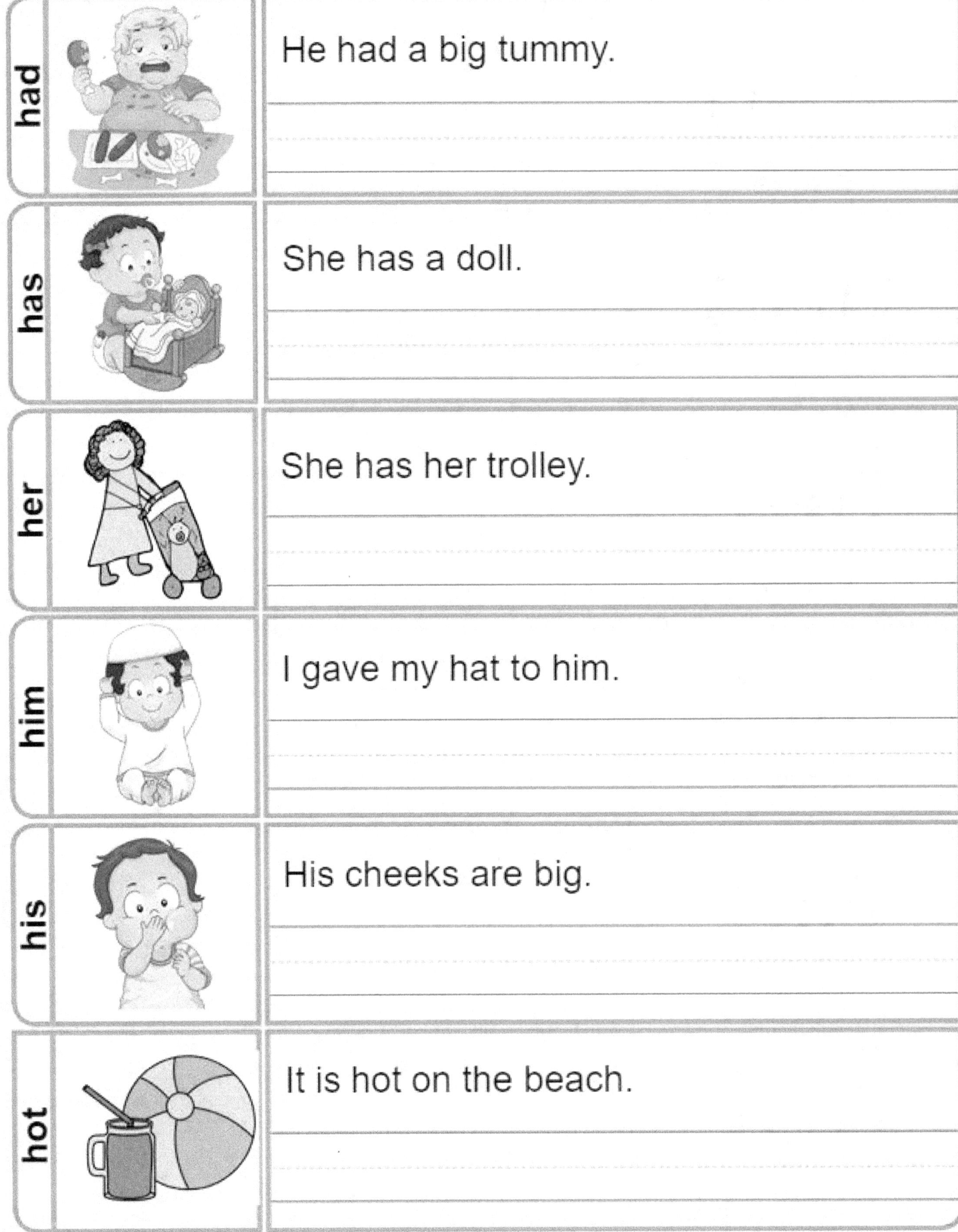

| |  |  |
|---|---|---|
| | **had** | He had a big tummy. |
| | **has** | She has a doll. |
| | **her** | She has her trolley. |
| | **him** | I gave my hat to him. |
| | **his** | His cheeks are big. |
| | **hot** | It is hot on the beach. |

| Read | Trace | Write |
| --- | --- | --- |
| **how** <br> hvordan | | |
| **its** <br> det er | | |
| **leg** <br> bein | | |
| **let** <br> la | | |
| **man** <br> mann | | |
| **may** <br> kan | | |

# Read and write the sentence!

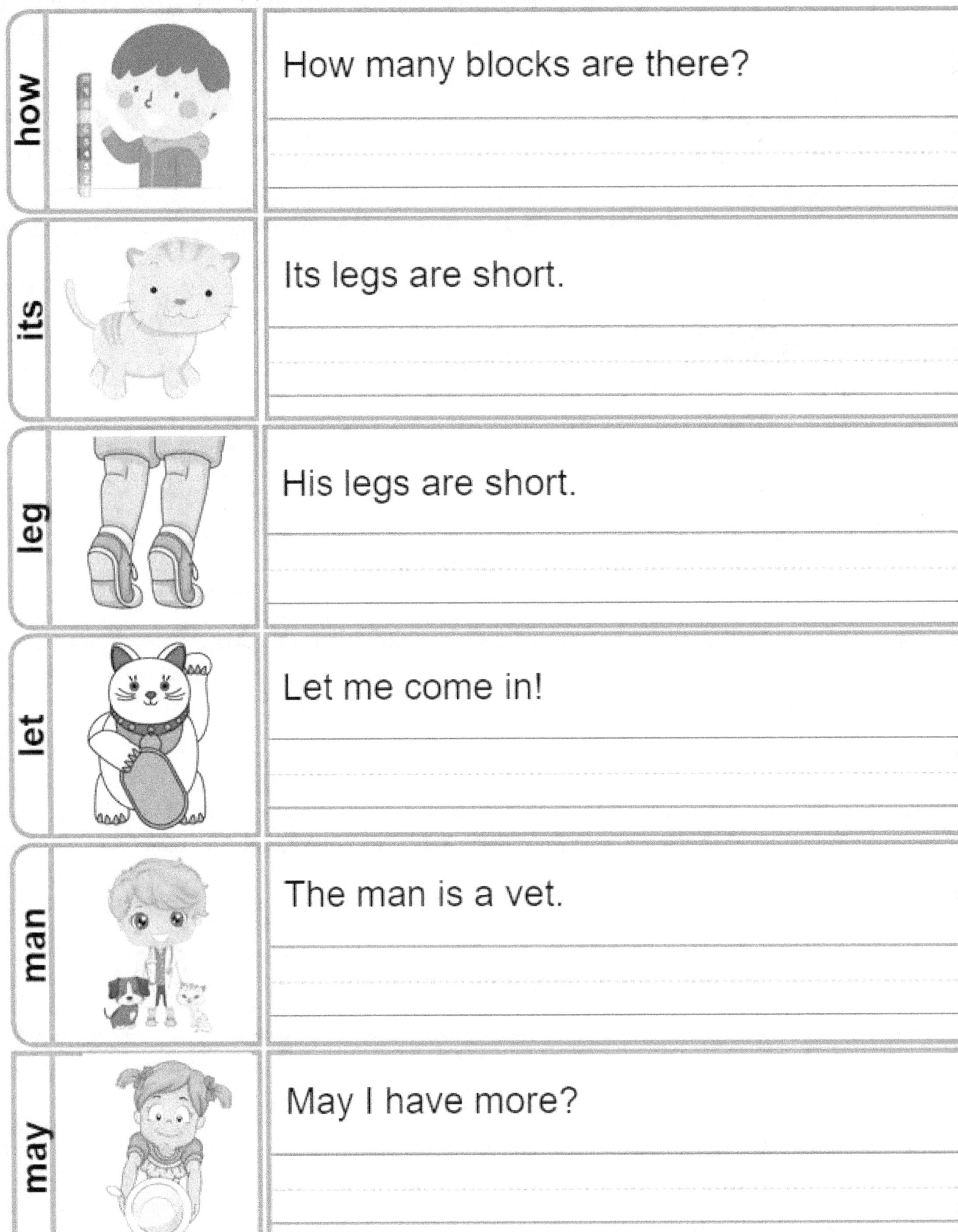

| how | How many blocks are there? |
| its | Its legs are short. |
| leg | His legs are short. |
| let | Let me come in! |
| man | The man is a vet. |
| may | May I have more? |

| Read | Trace | Write |
| --- | --- | --- |
| **men** <br> menn | men | |
| **new** <br> ny | new | |
| **not** <br> ikke | not | |
| **now** <br> nå | now | |
| **off** <br> av | off | |
| **old** <br> gammel | old | |

# Read and write the sentence!

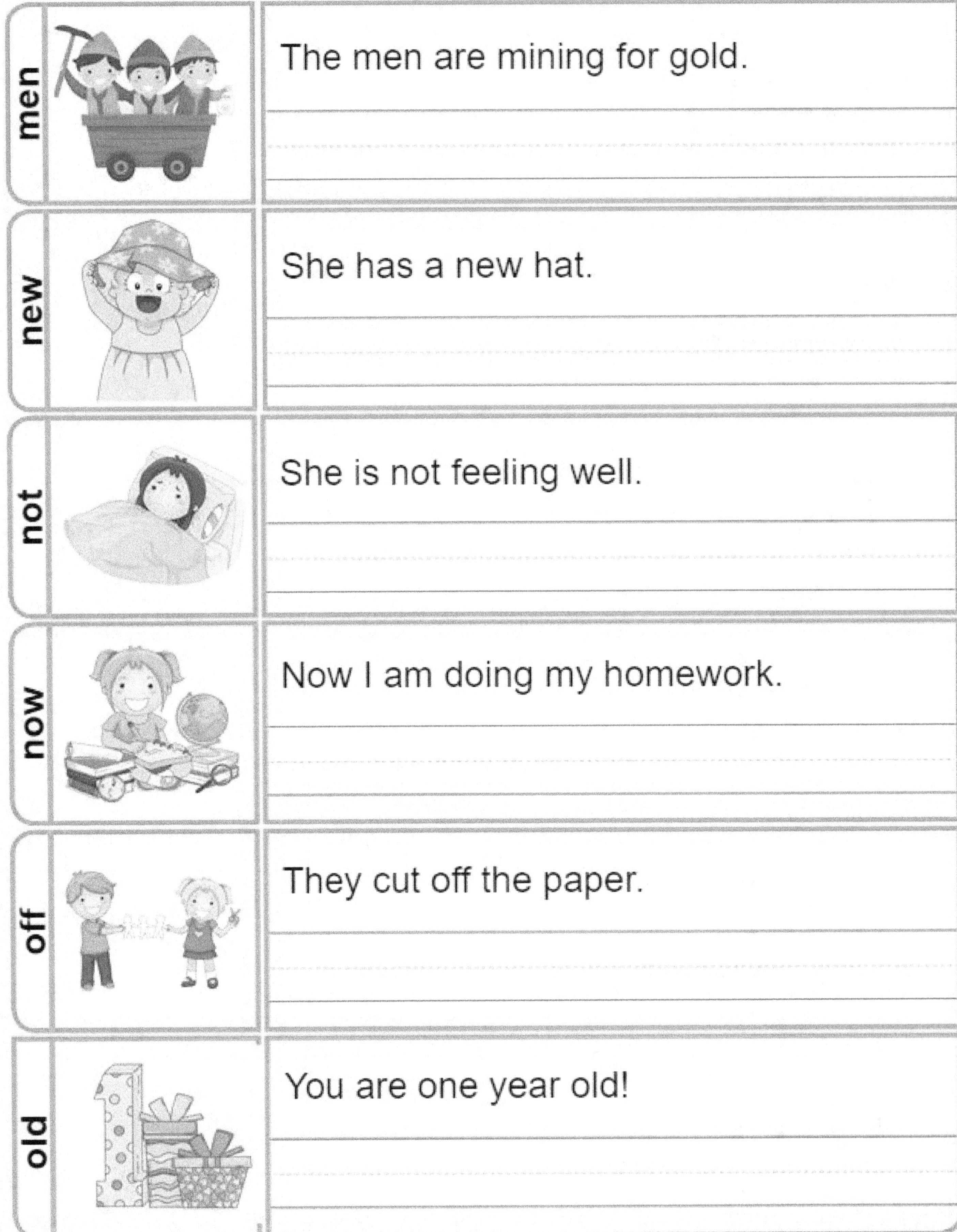

Read
Trace
Write
one
en
our
våre
out
ute
own
egen
pig
gris
put
sette

# Read and write the sentence!

| one | | The panda says one. |
| our | | This is our room. |
| out | | He will go out. |
| own | | The man owns a computer. |
| pig | | She is sleeping on her pig. |
| put | | She is putting an arm around her daughter. |

Read
Trace
Write
ran
løpe
red
rød
run
løpe
saw
se
say
si
see
se

# Read and write the sentence!

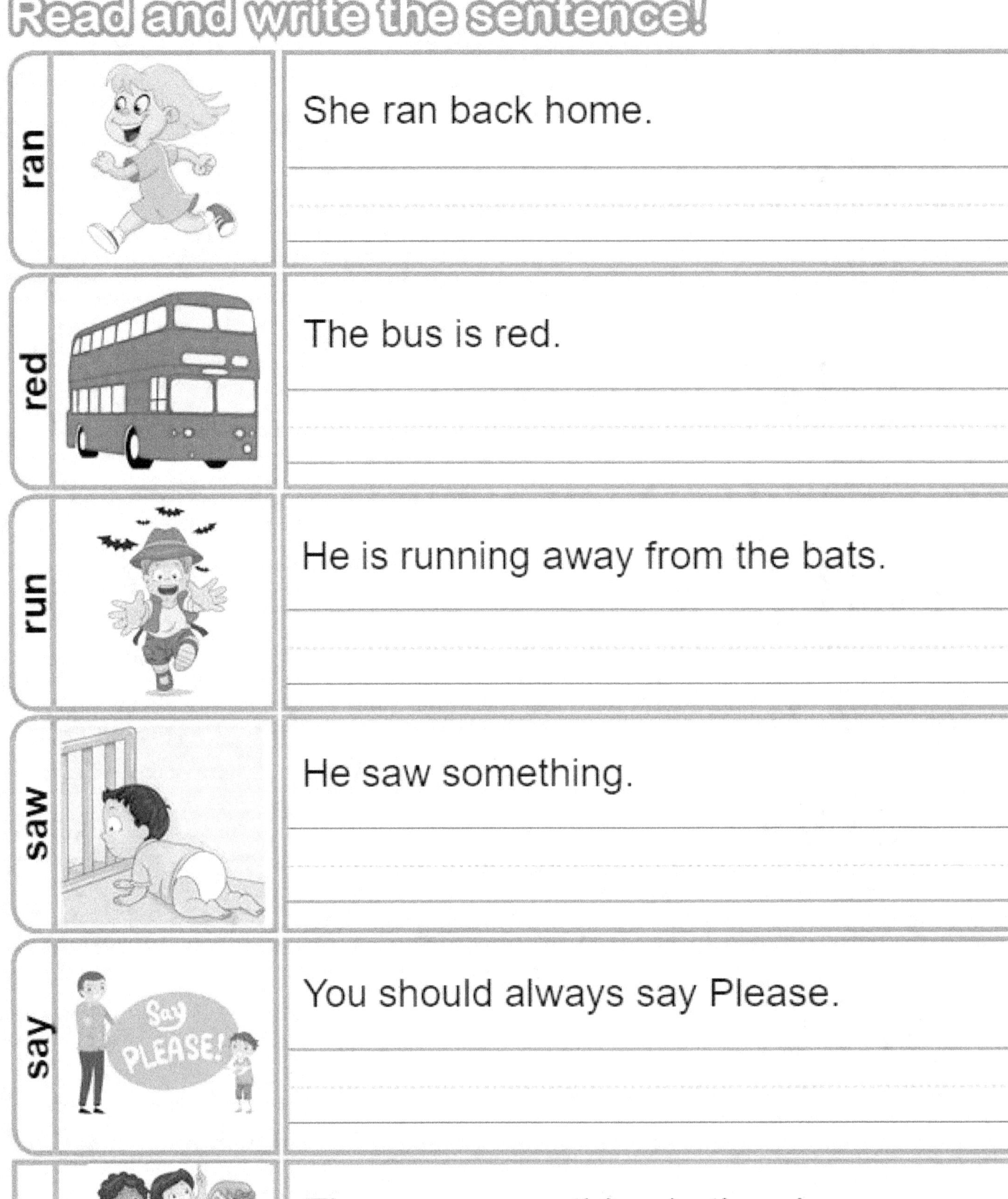

| Read | Trace | Write |
|---|---|---|

# Read and write the sentence!

Read
Trace
Write
too
også
top
topp
toy
leketøy
try
prøve
two
to
use
bruk

# Read and write the sentence!

Read
Trace
Write
was
var
way
vei
who
hva
why
hvorfor
yes
ja
you
du

# Read and write the sentence!

|  |  |
|------|----------|
| was | He was reading a book. |
| way | Let's go this way |
| who | Who wants to dance? |
| why | Why is the machine not working? |
| yes | Yes, I am so happy! |
| you | I love you! |

Read
Trace
Write
away
borte
baby
baby
back
tilbake
ball
ball
bear
bjørn
been
var

# Read and write the sentence!

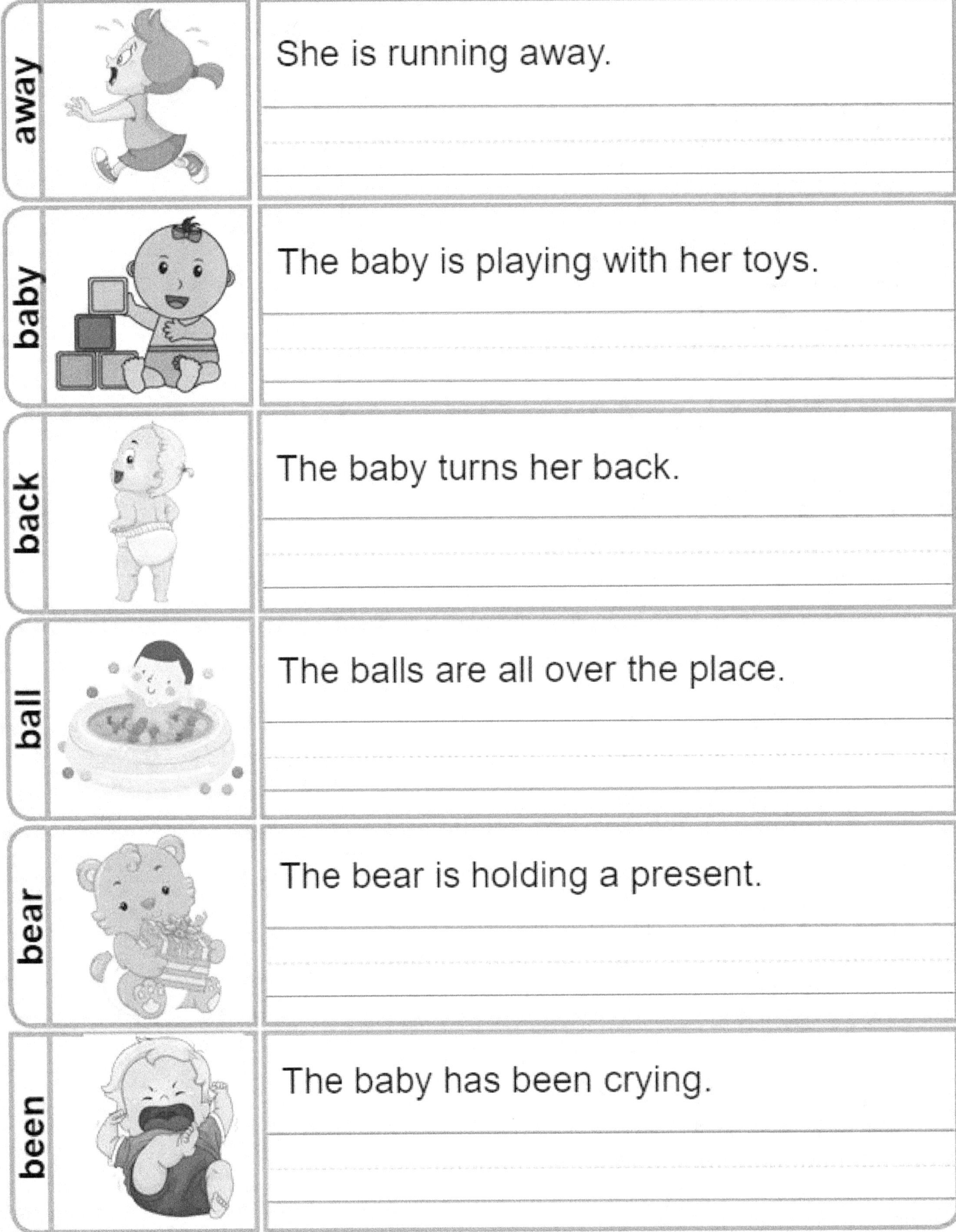

| Read | Trace | Write |
|------|-------|-------|
| **bell** <br> klokke | | |
| **best** <br> beste | | |
| **bird** <br> fugl | | |
| **blue** <br> blå | | |
| **boat** <br> båt | | |
| **both** <br> både | | |

# Read and write the sentence!

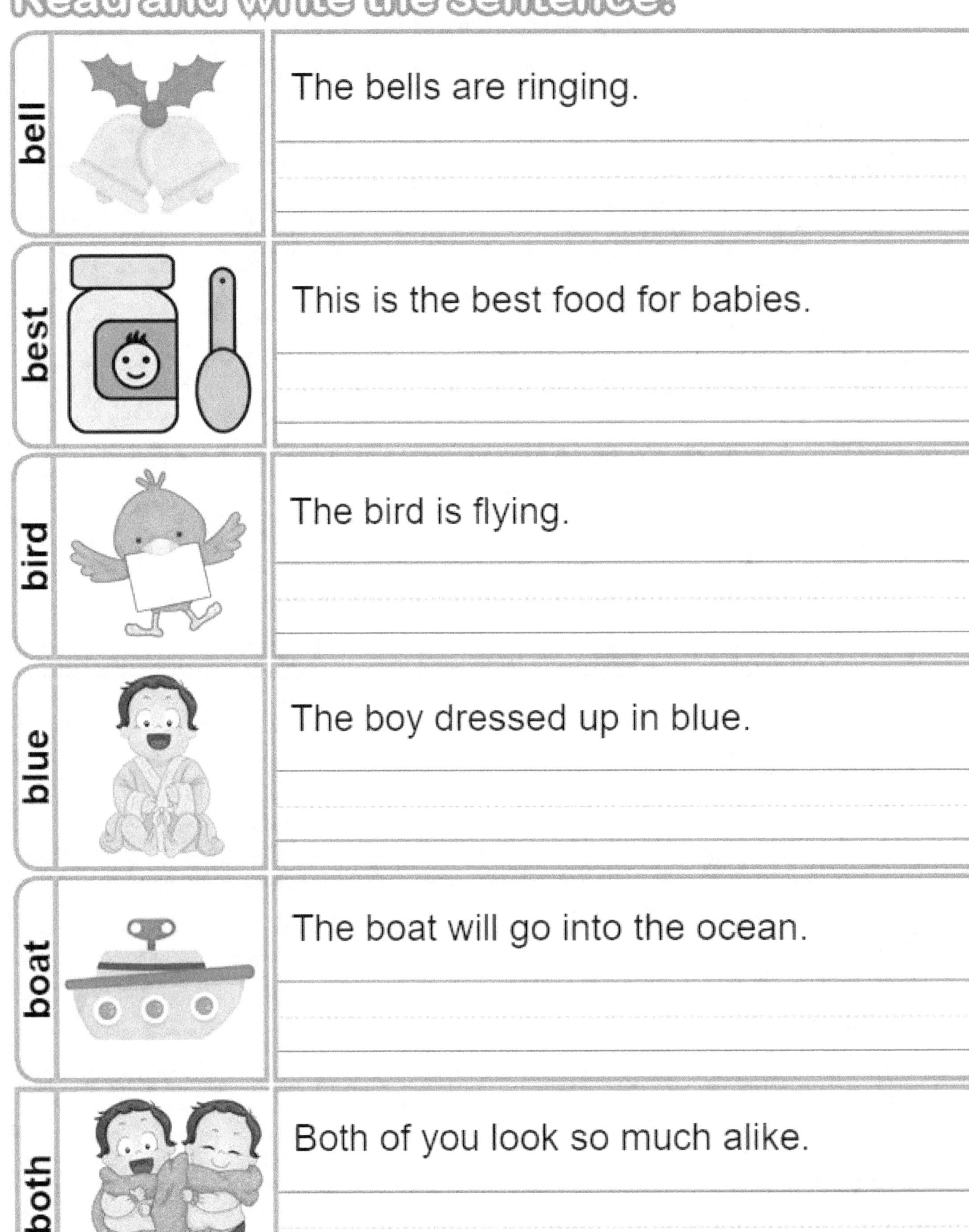

| | | |
|---|---|---|
| **bell** | | The bells are ringing. |
| **best** | | This is the best food for babies. |
| **bird** | | The bird is flying. |
| **blue** | | The boy dressed up in blue. |
| **boat** | | The boat will go into the ocean. |
| **both** | | Both of you look so much alike. |

| Read | Trace | Write |
| --- | --- | --- |
| **cake** <br> kake | | |
| **call** <br> anrop | | |
| **came** <br> kom | | |
| **coat** <br> frakk | | |
| **cold** <br> kald | | |
| **come** <br> komme | | |

# Read and write the sentence!

The cake is for your birthday.

She is calling for somebody.

She came with her bag.

The girl is wearing her coat.

The baby feels cold.

Come here to the slide!

| Read | Trace | Write |
| --- | --- | --- |
| **corn** <br> korn | | |
| **does** <br> gjør | | |
| **doll** <br> dukke | | |
| **done** <br> ferdig | | |
| **door** <br> dør | | |
| **down** <br> ned | | |

| | | |
|---|---|---|
| **corn** | | The corn tastes good. |
| **does** | | Does that thing taste bad? |
| **doll** | | She is hugging her doll. |
| **done** | | I've done reading my book. |
| **door** | | They open the door. |
| **down** | | The boy turns his head down. |

| Read | Trace | Write |
| --- | --- | --- |
| **draw** <br> tegne | | |
| **duck** <br> and | | |
| **fall** <br> falle | | |
| **farm** <br> gård | | |
| **fast** <br> rask | | |
| **feet** <br> fot | | |

# Read and write the sentence!

| draw | They all draw pictures. |
| duck | The duck is yellow. |
| fall | He fell down from the swing. |
| farm | He grows crops at his farm. |
| fast | She is doing everything very fast. |
| feet | I touch my feet. |

| Read | Trace | Write |
|------|-------|-------|
| **find**<br>finne | | |
| **fire**<br>brann | | |
| **fish**<br>fisk | | |
| **five**<br>fem | | |
| **four**<br>fire | | |
| **from**<br>fra | | |

# Read and write the sentence!

|  |  |
|------|----------|
| find | They are finding something. |
| fire | The fire is blazing and dangerous. |
| fish | The fish are swimming in the ocean. |
| five | You get birthday gifts for turning five. |
| four | The lion is turning four today. |
| from | She will draw a picture of her flower. |

Read
Trace
Write
full
full
game
spill
gave
ga
girl
pike
give
gi
goes
går

Read and write the sentence!

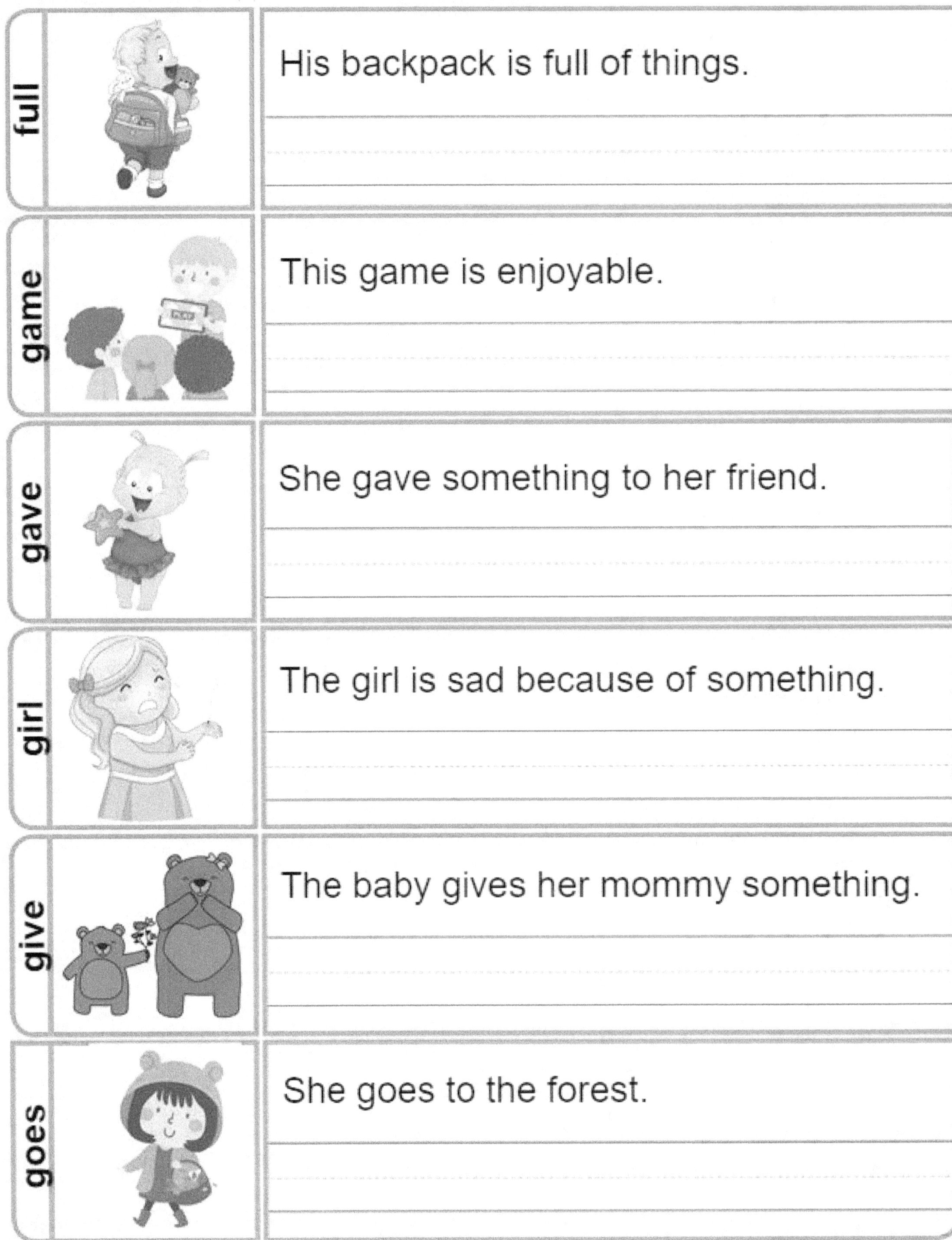

full

His backpack is full of things.

game

This game is enjoyable.

gave

She gave something to her friend.

girl

The girl is sad because of something.

give

The baby gives her mommy something.

goes

She goes to the forest.

Read
Trace
Write

good
flink

grow
vokse

hand
hånd

have
ha

head
hode

help
hjelp

# Read and write the sentence!

| good | The baby is acting very well today. |
| grow | My plant will grow! |
| hand | My hand is touching the wall. |
| have | She will have lots of friends. |
| head | My head is round. |
| help | They help each other wash the clothes. |

| Read | Trace | Write |
|------|-------|-------|
| here<br>her | | |
| hill<br>høyde | | |
| hold<br>holde | | |
| home<br>hjem | | |
| hurt<br>skade | | |
| into<br>inn i | | |

# Read and write the sentence!

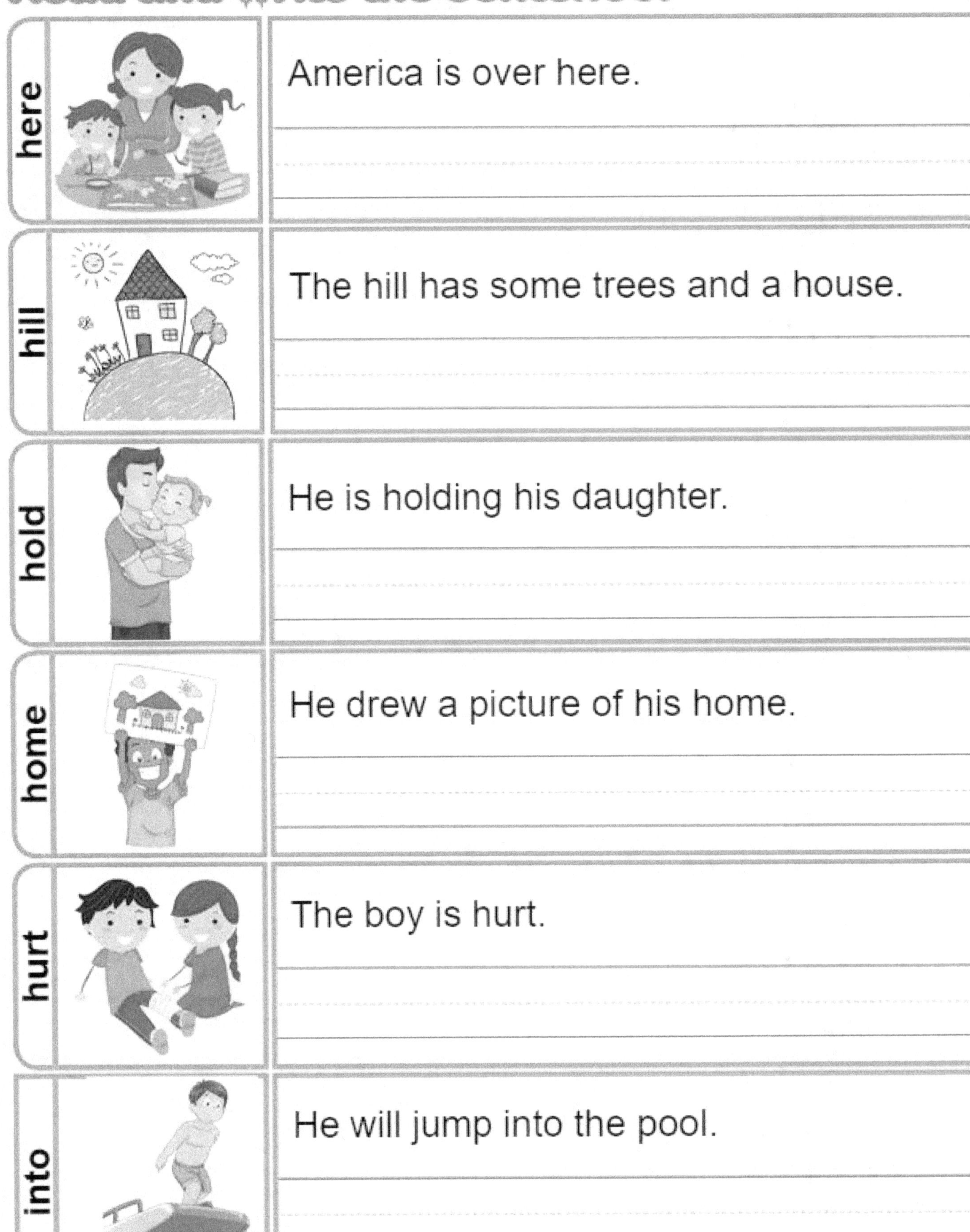

Read
Trace
Write
jump
hoppe
just
bare
keep
beholde
kind
snill
know
vet
like
som

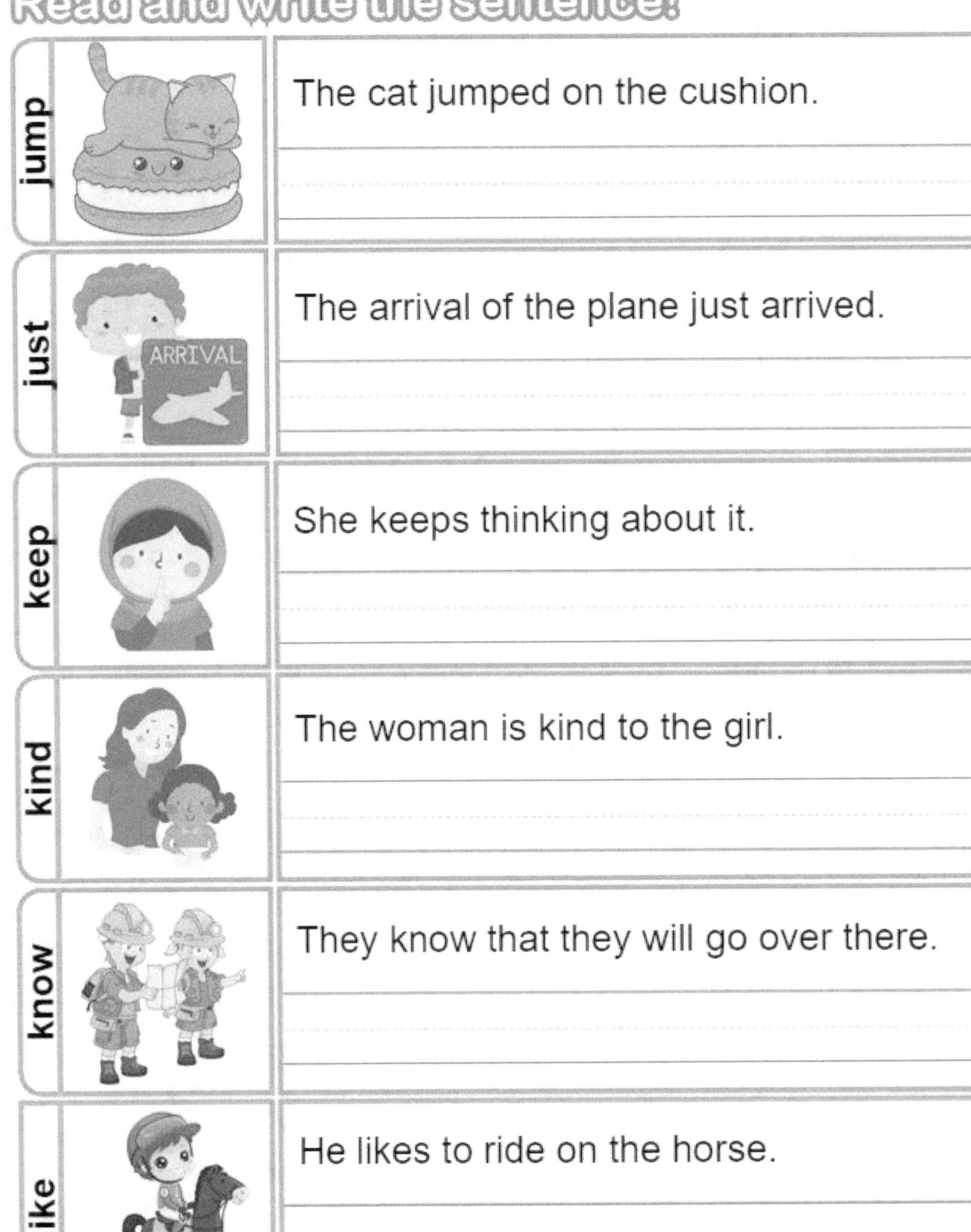


jump
The cat jumped on the cushion.
just
ARRIVAL
The arrival of the plane just arrived.
keep
She keeps thinking about it.
kind
The woman is kind to the girl.
know
They know that they will go over there.
like
He likes to ride on the horse.

Read
Trace
Write
live
bo
long
lang
look
se
made
laget
make
laget
many
mange

# Read and write the sentence!

|  |  |
|---|---|
| live | They all live together. |
| long | The pencil is very long. |
| look | They are looking at something. |
| made | They made a promise. |
| make | They are going to make something. |
| many | He has many shirts. |

Read
Trace
Write
milk
melk
much
mye
must
må
name
navn
nest
rede
once
en gang

# Read and write the sentence!

|  |  |
|---|---|
| milk | I have milk for breakfast. |
| much | I like to eat this very much. |
| must | I must do all my homework. |
| name | My name is Joe. |
| nest | The bird has a nest. |
| once | He once liked to look at his computer. |

Read
Trace
Write

only
bare

open
åpen

over
over

pick
plukke

play
spille

pull
dra

# Read and write the sentence!

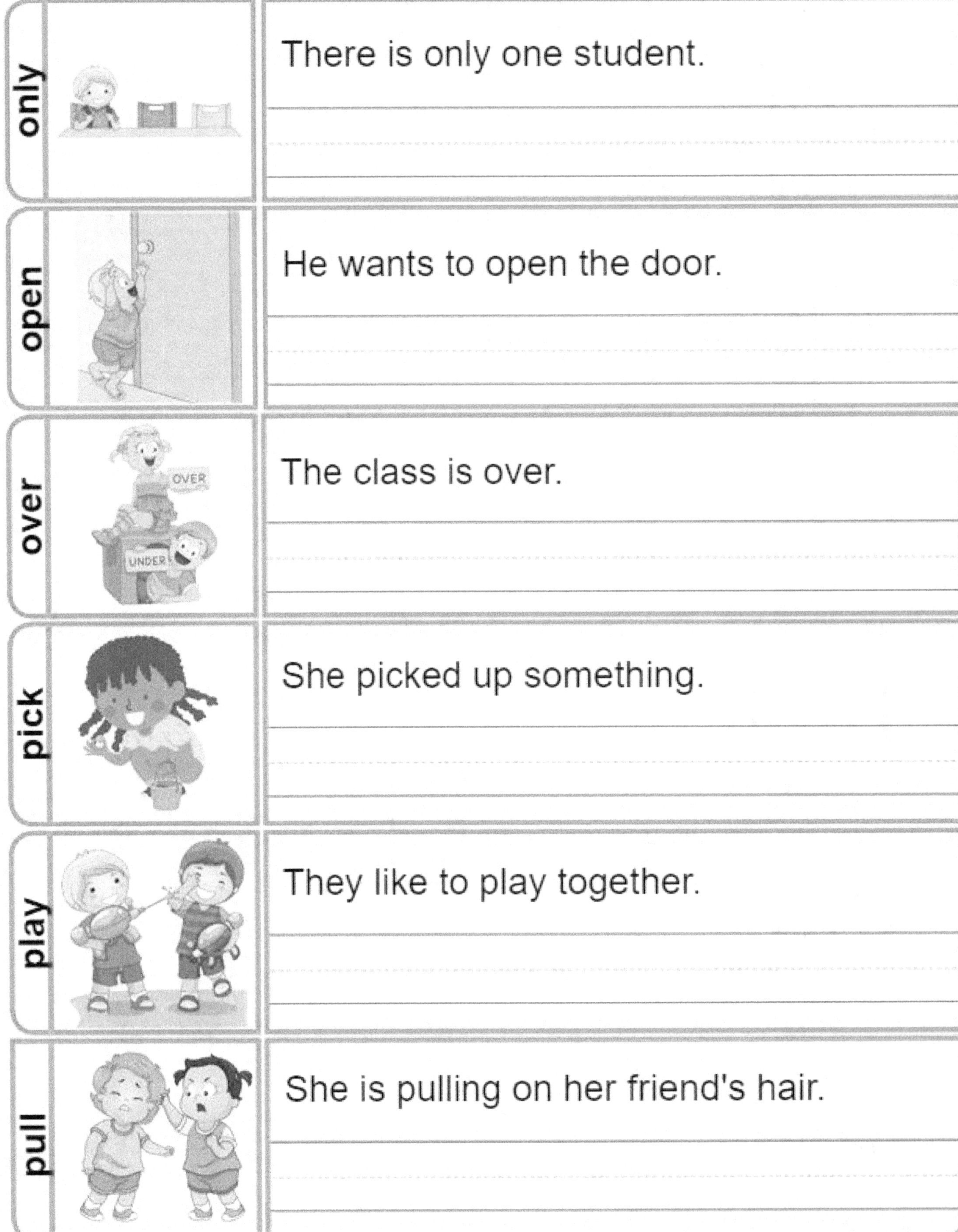

| Read | Trace | Write |
|---|---|---|
| rain<br>regn | | |
| read<br>lese | | |
| ride<br>ri | | |
| ring<br>ringe | | |
| said<br>sa | | |
| seed<br>frø | | |

# Read and write the sentence!

|  |  |
|---|---|
| rain | The rain is not going to hit us. |
| read | She likes to read books. |
| ride | The baby is riding on a toy horse. |
| ring | The bird is holding a ring in its beak. |
| said | She said hello to her neighbor. |
| seed | The seeds are going to plant. |

Read
Trace
Write
shoe
sko
show
forestilling
sing
synge
snow
snø
some
noen
song
sang

# Read and write the sentence!

| shoe | Her shoes are cute and purple. |
| show | This map shows the location. |
| sing | The baby can sing along. |
| snow | I like to play snow. |
| some | These are some of my toys. |
| song | I will sing a song in the talent show. |

Read
Trace
Write
soon
snart
stop
stoppe
take
ta
tell
fortelle
that
at
them
dem

| | | |
|---|---|---|
| **soon** |  | The eggs will hatch soon. |
| **stop** |  | The teacher says to stop. |
| **take** |  | They take some flowers. |
| **tell** |  | She is telling a story. |
| **that** |  | That bird dressed up as Santa. |
| **them** | | He likes to eat them. |

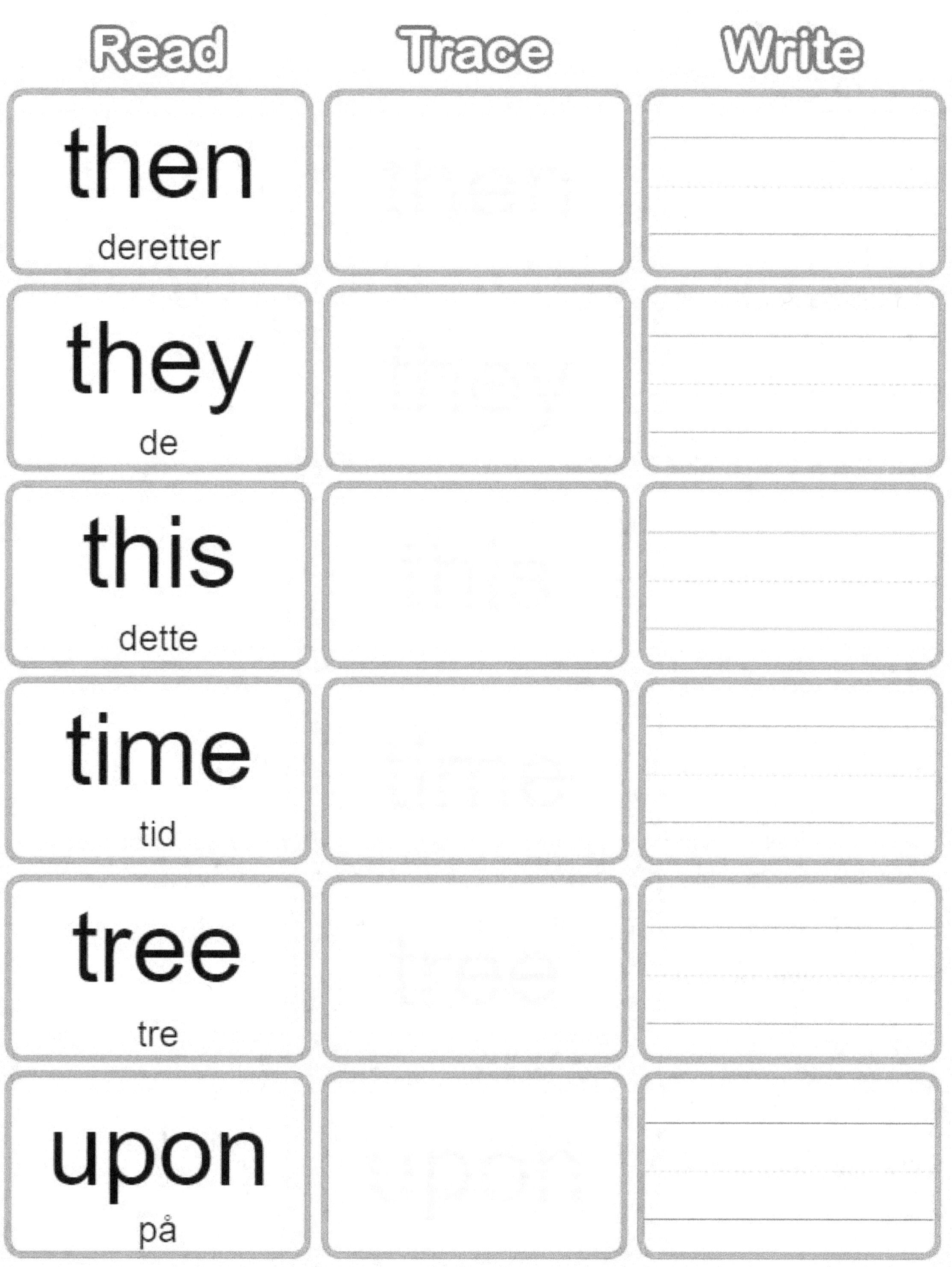

Read
Trace
Write
then
deretter
they
de
this
dette
time
tid
tree
tre
upon
på

# Read and write the sentence!

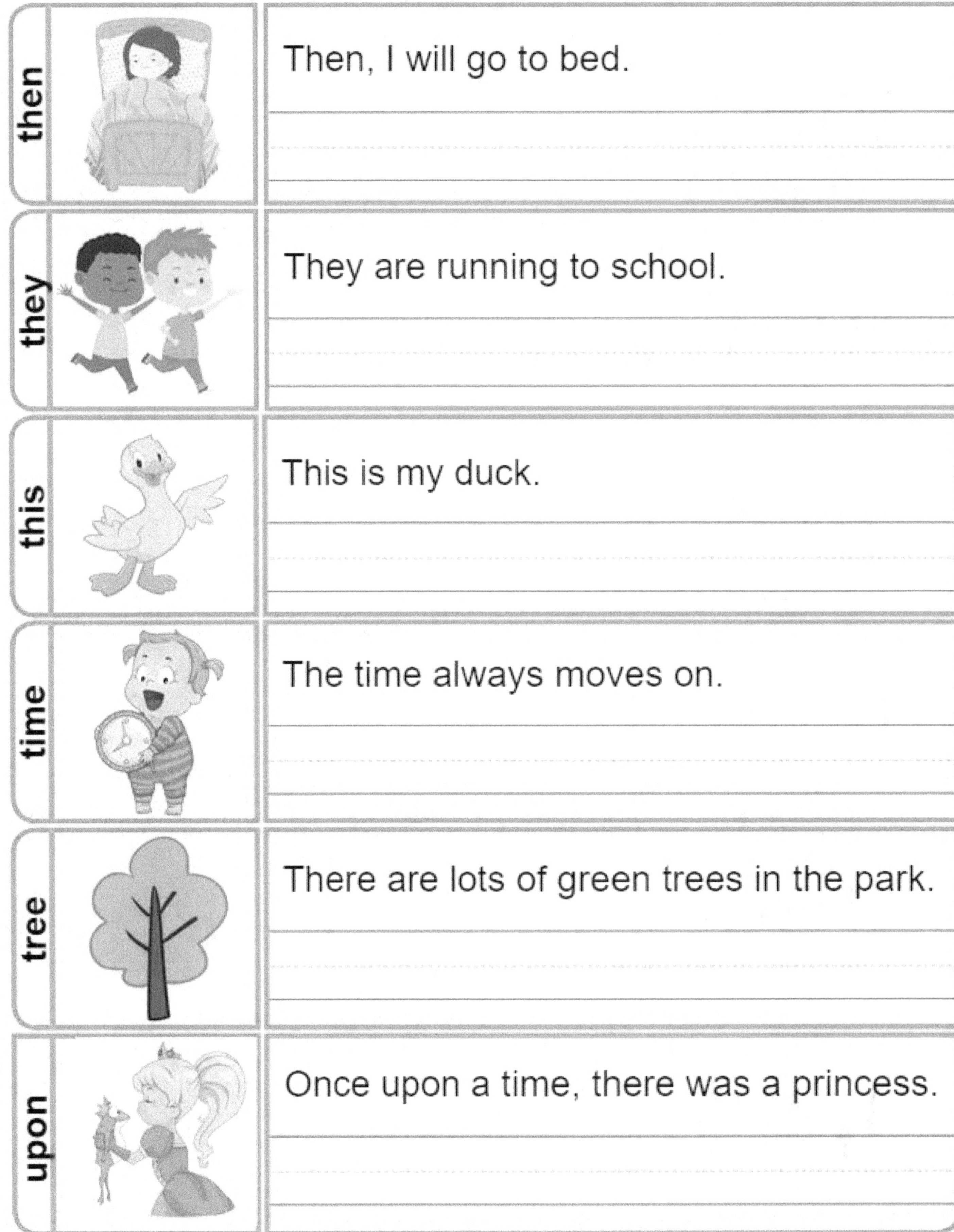

| Read | Trace | Write |
| --- | --- | --- |
| **very** <br> veldig | | |
| **walk** <br> gå | | |
| **want** <br> vil | | |
| **warm** <br> varm | | |
| **wash** <br> vask | | |
| **well** <br> vi vil | | |

# Read and write the sentence!

| very | | The baby is lovely. |
| walk | | They are walking on the sidewalk. |
| want | | The baby wants more milk. |
| warm | | The bath is warm. |
| wash | | She is going to wash the dishes. |
| well | | He can save money well. |

Read
Trace
Write
went
gikk
were
er
what
hva
when
når
will
vil
wind
vind

# Read and write the sentence!

| | | |
|---|---|---|
| **went** | | The crocodile went to the pond. |
| **were** | | There were lots of toys. |
| **what** | | What is the lion doing? |
| **when** | | When are you going to wake up? |
| **will** | | Will I get it in? |
| **wind** | | The wind is blowing fiercely. |

Read
Trace
Write
wish
håp
with
med
wood
tre
work
arbeid
your
din
about
om

# Read and write the sentence!

| | | |
|---|---|---|
| **wish** | | I wish you a happy Christmas! |
| **with** | | He is with his sister. |
| **wood** | | He is stacking up wooden blocks. |
| **work** | | He is going to work in his tractor. |
| **your** | | Your baby is wearing a yellow suit. |
| **about** |  | It's about to be 12:30. |

Read
Trace
Write
after
etter
again
en gang til
apple
eple
black
svart
bread
brød
bring
bringe

# Read and write the sentence!

|  | |  |
|---|---|---|
| after | | The teacher calmed them after they fought. |
| again | | He did it again! |
| apple | | The apple is red and juicy. |
| black | | The crow is black. |
| bread | | My breakfast is bread and jam. |
| bring | | He is bringing his project. |

<table>
<tr><th>Read</th><th>Trace</th><th>Write</th></tr>
<tr><td>brown<br>brun</td><td></td><td></td></tr>
<tr><td>carry<br>bære</td><td></td><td></td></tr>
<tr><td>chair<br>stol</td><td></td><td></td></tr>
<tr><td>clean<br>ren</td><td></td><td></td></tr>
<tr><td>could<br>kan</td><td></td><td></td></tr>
<tr><td>don't<br>ikke</td><td></td><td></td></tr>
</table>

# Read and write the sentence!

| brown | | Her stuffed animal is a brown bear. |
| carry | | He is carrying a big crayon. |
| chair | | He is sitting on his chair. |
| clean | | He needs to clean up. |
| could | | The baby could do push-ups. |
| don't | | Don't do that! |

| Read | Trace | Write |
| --- | --- | --- |
| **drink**<br>drikke | | |
| **eight**<br>åtte | | |
| **every**<br>hver | | |
| **first**<br>først | | |
| **floor**<br>gulv | | |
| **found**<br>funnet | | |

# Read and write the sentence!

| drink | The baby likes to drink water. |
| eight | You get eight gifts for turning eight! |
| every | Every book is colorful. |
| first | We won first place. |
| floor | She is sitting on the floor. |
| found | It found a hat in the streets. |

| Read | Trace | Write |
| --- | --- | --- |
| funny<br>morsom | | |
| going<br>gå | | |
| grass<br>gress | | |
| green<br>grønn | | |
| horse<br>hest | | |
| house<br>hus | | |

# Read and write the sentence!

| funny | The rabbit thinks the joke is funny. |
| going | The bear is going to eat all the honey. |
| grass | The goat eats grass on the hill. |
| green | The turtle that is walking is green. |
| horse | The horse is magical. |
| house | They lived in that house. |

Read
Trace
Write
kitty
katt
laugh
latter
light
lys
money
penger
never
aldri
night
natt

# Read and write the sentence!

| kitty | The kitties are charming. |
| laugh | They are laughing while playing. |
| light | The boy will turn on the lights. |
| money | I have earned a lot of money. |
| never | The bear never ate ice cream before. |
| night | I will sleep on my blanket at night. |

Read
Trace
Write
paper
papir
party
parti
right
riktig
round
rund
seven
sju
shall
skal

# Read and write the sentence!

Read
Trace
Write
sheep
sau
sleep
sove
small
liten
start
start
stick
pinner
table
bord

Read and write the sentence!


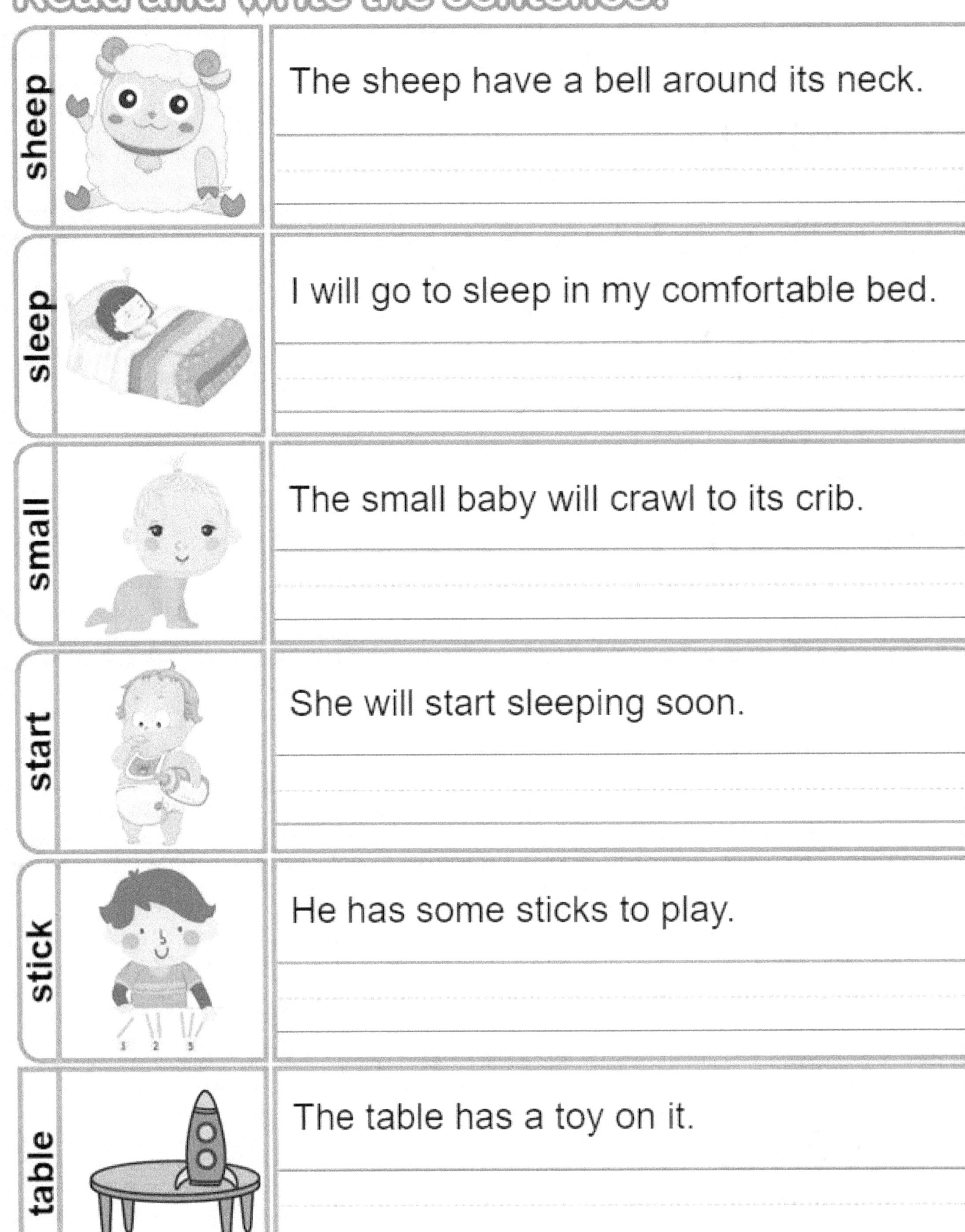


sheep
The sheep have a bell around its neck.

sleep
I will go to sleep in my comfortable bed.

small
The small baby will crawl to its crib.

start
She will start sleeping soon.

stick
He has some sticks to play.

table
The table has a toy on it.

Read
Trace
Write

thank
takke

their
deres

there
der

these
disse

thing
ting

think
synes at

| | |
|---|---|
| **thank** | He made a Thank you card for you. |
| **their** | They will enjoy their picnic. |
| **there** | There is something in front of you. |
| **these** | These are my eating material. |
| **thing** | The thing is broken. |
| **think** | She thinks about what she is going to draw. |

Read
Trace
Write
those
de
three
tre
today
i dag
under
under
watch
se
water
vann

# Read and write the sentence!

|  |  |
|------|----------|
| those | Those are mine. |
| three | She will turn three today. |
| today | Today is a beautiful day. |
| under | The puppy sleeps under the blanket. |
| watch | They both watch the video. |
| water | He is drinking water after a long soccer game. |

| Read | Trace | Write |
| --- | --- | --- |
| **where** <br> hvor | | |
| **which** <br> hvilken | | |
| **white** <br> hvit | | |
| **would** <br> ville | | |
| **write** <br> skrive | | |
| **always** <br> bestandig | | |

# Read and write the sentence!

| | |
|---|---|
| **where**  | Where are we? |
| **which**  | The clothes which are my sisters are colorful. |
| **white**  | The sheep have white wool. |
| **would**  | He would tell them a story. |
| **write**  | I like to write lots of stories. |
| **always** | I am always happy that it is Christmas. |

| Read | Trace | Write |
| --- | --- | --- |
| **around**<br>rundt | | |
| **before**<br>før | | |
| **better**<br>bedre | | |
| **farmer**<br>bonde | | |
| **father**<br>far | | |
| **flower**<br>blomst | | |

# Read and write the sentence!

| around | I will shuffle the shapes around. |
| before | Before I go to school, I kiss my mom. |
| better | I can make it better. |
| farmer | The farmer takes care of the animals. |
| father | My father is wearing a blue shirt. |
| flower | She will play with the flowers. |

| Read | Trace | Write |
| --- | --- | --- |
| garden<br>hage | | |
| ground<br>bakke | | |
| letter<br>bokstaver | | |
| little<br>litt | | |
| mother<br>mor | | |
| myself<br>meg selv | | |

# Read and write the sentence!

**garden** — Her garden is vast and healthy.

**ground** — I am playing with my dog on the ground.

**letter** — These are the letters A, B, and C.

**little** — The world is small.

**mother** — My mother is very nice.

**myself** — I made these by myself.

Read
Trace
Write

please
vær så snill

pretty
ganske

rabbit
kanin

school
skole

sister
søster

street
gate

# Read and write the sentence!

| | | |
|---|---|---|
| **please** | | Please stop pulling my hair. |
| **pretty** | | She made the cake very pretty. |
| **rabbit** | | The rabbit is white and soft. |
| **school** | | This is the school. |
| **sister** |  | My sister is wearing a pink dress. |
| **street** |  | They are walking across the street. |

| Read | Trace | Write |
|---|---|---|
| **window**<br>vindu | | |
| **yellow**<br>gul | | |
| **because**<br>fordi | | |
| **brother**<br>bror | | |
| **chicken**<br>kylling | | |
| **goodbye**<br>ha det | | |

# Read and write the sentence!

| | | |
|---|---|---|
| window |  | The window is open. |
| yellow |  | The ducky is yellow. |
| because |  | She will sleep because it is night. |
| brother |  | His brother is playing with him. |
| chicken |  | The chicken has hatched out of the egg. |
| goodbye |  | The animal is saying goodbye. |

| Read | Trace | Write |
| --- | --- | --- |
| **morning** <br> morgen | | |
| **picture** <br> bilde | | |
| **birthday** <br> fødselsdag | | |
| **children** <br> barn | | |
| **squirrel** <br> ekorn | | |
| **together** <br> sammen | | |

# Read and write the sentence!

| morning | He likes to ride his bike in the morning. |
| picture | He will take a picture. |
| birthday | Today is my birthday! |
| children | The children are doing something. |
| squirrel | The squirrel is cute. |
| together | They are sharing a bed together. |